LEAN TOWARD THE LIGHT

poems by

Geoffrey Godbey

Finishing Line Press
Georgetown, Kentucky

LEAN TOWARD THE LIGHT

Copyright © 2024 by Geoffrey Godbey
ISBN 979-8-88838-426-8 First Edition
All rights reserved under International and Pan-American Copyright Conventions. No part of this book may be reproduced in any manner whatsoever without written permission from the publisher, except in the case of brief quotations embodied in critical articles and reviews.

ACKNOWLEDGMENTS

These poems are a recognition that poetry is a gift. I have not tried to publish most of them, although the process to do so is known by heart. The only justification for writing them is that I must. Most are shaped by the age at which I have arrived, broken and sparkling. It is now possible, and necessary, to see the extraordinary beauty of the world, and confess how much of it we have forfeited. More than ever, we must lean toward the light.

Some of my poems have appeared in *The Nation, Malahat Review, Westigan Review, Pembroke Magazine, Pivot, Northwest Review, Congress II*—re-printed in *Zero Makes Me Hungry—A Collection of Poems for Today*. New York: Scott Foresman, *Reflections*, New York: Scott Foresman, *Remove the Blindfold: Book 2*. Toronto: Oxford University Press, Canada, *State College Magazine, The Little Magazine, The Small Pond, The World and I*, and *Twelve Festival Poets*, edited by Deborah Austin, Jack McManis, and Sandra Nestlerode. State College, PA: Central Pennsylvania Festival of the Arts. "All That Jazz" won the Bellefonte PA Art Museum poetry contest in 2023.There are also lots of Facebook followers.

Publisher: Leah Huete de Maines
Editor: Christen Kincaid
Cover Art: Madame Lalune by Nella Godbey Storm
Author Photo: Ken Noel Photography, State College, PA
Cover Design: Elizabeth Maines McCleavy

Order online: www.finishinglinepress.com
also available on amazon.com

Author inquiries and mail orders:
Finishing Line Press
PO Box 1626
Georgetown, Kentucky 40324
USA

Contents

Hello 1
Fragments 3
The Day Goes Down 5
A life 6
Kite and String 7
Thumb 9
The Rock Finally Speaks 11
The Ways of Water 12
Another Small String of Ironies 13
Along For the Ride 15
Willow and Jay 16
She Can Mend 17
Of Course 18
Mourning Dove 19
This Place 20
Some Colors 21
October 23
Muse Re-Visited 24
Ridges 25
Cold Sun 26
If Ever 27
Turnip 28
Rain 29
China Flight 30
Clothes in A Chest of Drawers 31
November 10 32
Can You Gargle 33
All That Jazz 34

B. Baxter Bear Boy	35
Finally	36
Old Trees	37
Seven A.M. Rain	38
October	39
Good News	30
Grief	41
The Snow	42
Merwin	43
On My Property	44
The Day	46
Blue Tide Turning	47
Photosynthesis	48
Barn Light	49
Firefly	50
Diamond Water	51
I Wish for You	52
Summer Fragments	53
Where	54
Mermaid	55
Driving Home in the Dark	56
We Are Held	58
Visitor	59
Suppose	60
Long Time Coming	61
Memory	62

To all that I love without effort

HELLO

Hello to the things
that cannot answer back.
Hello to the past,
plunging in its
blue sea of nostalgia.

Hello to hope,
stranger that
wants us to follow.

Hello to women,
I have finally
paid attention
and say a late hello
like an awe-struck child.

Hello to those who
thought they were
the rulers,
swimming in their
own ego.
Drowning
with open mouths.

Hello to Hollywood,
but I was never
that desperate.

Hello to the small,
to the vague,
to the tree that
will not burn.
The reluctant mouse
on heaven's highway.

Hello to those who
learn at
the great cost
of certainty.

Hello to whatever
wants
to return hello.

Hello to darkness
and returning echo.
God's voice
in a cave,
which sounds a little
like our own.

Hello.

FRAGMENTS

1.
2:00 A.M.
ghost dog
barking
three hills over
half a dream away.

2.
What made
a path
through wet
morning grass?

3.
My bad ears
miss
some sounds
but always hear
the closing
of doors.

4.
Pour
a bucket
of patience
over
my restlessness.

5.
Recognize
the feast.

6.
Insects.
Kings in exile.

7.
The circle finds
it is its

own ancestor.
The straight line
finds it cannot
go back home.

8.
Here is a test
to be taken
on what
the twilight
has discovered.

9.
Child's sparkler
in darkness.

10.
Even if I left
my voice
it would not
leave me.

11.
Kiss
the pain
beyond words
joy
beyond words
of this vast
spinning place.

THE DAY GOES DOWN

The day goes down
knowing the way.

The day, we think,
is our measure;
not the week
or sudden years.
But the day knows
none of that.

Dreams and directions
lag behind
what we have become
like a dead maple tree
remembering sun

or a rain drop
still in love
with the cloud
it falls away from.

Insistent voice
finally reaching
an empty room
with some
just discovered vision.

But the day goes down
knowing the way.
It is a long way.

Blind spark
lights the same trail.

It is a long way.

A LIFE

What if I came down
out of those
solid dark clouds
that build up
against the mountains
day after day
with no rain in them
and lived as
one blade of grass
in a garden
in the south
when the clouds
part late in winter.

From the beginning
I would be older
than the animals
and to the last
I would be simpler.

Frost would design me
and dew would
disappear on me.
Sun would
shine through me.

I would be green
with white roots.
Feel worms
touch my feet
with joy.
Have no name
and no fear.
Turn naturally
toward the light.
Know how to spend
days and nights
climbing out of myself
all my life.

KITE AND STRING

I always thought
men were the kites
women were the strings
allowing our jump and bob
flight to success,
holding against
the Icarus wing-flap
toward the sun
that so often kills
the unattended male.
Children were also
tiny kites
on a string
exploring the vast world,
slowly if lucky,
by looking down at it,
not up.

I was a kite,
jumping toward
the limits
while knowing I was
held from harm
the path cleared
meals lined up like
so many tiny soldiers
marching toward
my success.
Lurch and glide,
tail in your face
from sudden downdraft
and the endless climb,
just as I was
told it should be.
I climbed from
the pressure of that.
Success the snap
that cut the kite adrift
in the uncaring universe

and I found
I was really
the string
snaking down
toward
the cold earth
and the kite
was a woman
navigating the sky.

No need for
the infinite climb.

THUMB

When you quit
sucking on it
you forgot it.
But the thumbs
did not forget you.

Whatever you held
up to the light
the barely noticed
thumb
held it from harm
against the helpless fingers.

The fingers like
Cinderella's sisters.
Pointer finger amazed
it could form a circle
with the help
of the thumb.
Middle finger always
with an anger
management problem.
Ring finger useless
but decorated
and the pinkie
just out there and
friendless.

Hitchhiking
you aimed the thumb
toward the future
and when the stranger's car
pulled off the road
up ahead you
walked briskly toward it.
Thumb already
in your pocket.

Thumbs up or down
was how we signal
the fate of things.
(even this poem).

Every plate, tennis racquet,
sheet of paper,
glass of wine
needed the thumb.

Thumb like a housewife
never appreciated
until she simply left
one day
her note saying
no more, no more.
The fingers gathering
like an emergency meeting
of the UN.
What the hell
do we do now.

THE ROCK FINALLY SPEAKS

I was here
when the ancestors
of your ancestors
opened their eyes
to the phantasmagoria
of existence
and I stayed silent
waiting for the
right time.

Sleeping in fields
and lonely mountains.
Knowing what I knew
from the beginning.
If a rock ever changes
it will begin to disappear
so, my speaking to you
means my end.
You cannot
waste words
if you are a rock.
Once and done.
My voice deeper
than you can hear.

I say only
I have never
needed to know
what cannot
be known.

I have always
been here
for whatever
comes next.

THE WAYS OF WATER

Wondrous
ways
the water
works
its will.

Flood, flume
and falls,
tide turning
toward itself.

Drips, drops
the dam
that drowns
but we notice
water only
as it shows
it does not
need us.

Tide turns
torrents
trail away
like a
child's balloon
that climbs the sky
even as
the child
regrets
ignoring
the string.

ANOTHER SMALL STRING OF IRONIES

You have not
wasted your life
but your life,
against its will,
has wasted you.

You. talk
to a dog
mostly
about things
you cannot smell.

You have what it takes
it takes what you have.

The birds, our friends,
leave us
white spots,
old feathers
and go south.

We are so often cold
but the largest fire
that ever existed
finds us most mornings.

The future can dance
without having to
choose a partner.

Your dreams
put their weight
on the scales
but since they fly
the scales do not react.

My father ended a poem,
so long ago,
about the world;

"Here, as we must,
live on the narrow rim
of the sun.
It is sufficient.
Turn to me now
that thinking is done."

ALONG FOR THE RIDE

I have become
Director of Trees,
Superintendent of the Sky.

I have become harmless;
a lot for a man.

I eat good stuff
and the wind promises
no more mischief from
its old urge.

I have become
a happy man;
the futures market
for self-pity
down based on evidence...

folks who love me.

Numb sequence of life
that runs so well
without us.

Without me.

Just along for the ride.

What a ride.

What a big fat
lost long ride.

WILLOW AND JAY

Why did the Blue Jay
fly from the feeder
to the highest branch
of the old willow,
bald in November,
leaves shed for
the last time?

Perhaps
the willow
called to him
with its whole life.

SHE CAN MEND

For Barbara

She can mend
the broken moment.

Jumpstart joy from
its low slumber.

She can fuse
the fractured future.

Fuss at chaos.
Order random color.

Frame it off
for light to find it.

She can clutch
the least day's leavings

all it came with
claim and tame it.

She holds what
old hills have told her.

She can mend
the broken moment.

OF COURSE

The first
finger of grass
greens and wakens
knowing there
is nothing
to tell this
turning to.

Twisting away
from the cold.

Seeing possibilities
down the
frozen ridge
when whatever
is under the earth
turns and sighs
at the next round
of life
when the
just-born flies,
not knowing why,
will dance
and test the air.

MOURNING DOVE

This mourning dove
looks the same
as the others
until it walks
the back deck.

One foot is gone.

Peg-legged it gimps
the area where
seeds have filtered down
to those who
know their place
but in my moment
of sympathy
it smacks my mind.

Sudden flight
toward some
high place.
It flies
and flies
in perfect grace.

THIS PLACE

Walking the field
I belong to
no less than
the Queen Annes Lace.

Over on the interstate
cars sing
into the wind,
trucks howl
like some animal
near extinction.

Garden teaching me
its old song,

garlic growing
stronger than life.

Sycamore waving
to an
unseen friend.

Ghost deer,
intruder squirrel,
warrior sparrow.

Alone and together
with the one
I love.

Sun and moon
interchangeable balls
for the sport
of the universe.

My life measured
by their game;
my time
by their travels.

SOME COLORS

Olive

Take the soil
 beneath the ground
 and the grass above it.
Squeeze them together
in strong, weathered hands.

Blue

We started together
but some of us
ran into the night
while others rose
weightless
into the air
expectant
and innocent
so now
we cannot
recognize
our family.

Purple

Ancient royal line
a single strain
slowly weakened from
its vaulted heritage
and in the shadows
of long hallways
desire
is pacing about.

Brown

I was like
the youngest child
whose birthday

is forgotten
but will live
so much longer
than the others.

White

All bad deeds
go unpunished.
You cannot punish
what you
cannot see.

OCTOBER

The dark
arrives
more easily
as the sun
loses interest.

October
in the
wings
of birds.

Final glory.

We,
owning nothing
but the
scent of change.

The coming cold
that does not
remember
who we are.

The coming heat
that will not
remember
who we were.

We who
were supposed
to be
everything.

Helpless in the
kingdom of change.

MUSE RE-VISITED

Turns out to be a plump guy,
balding, stubble-faced,
in a pink tutu and ballet slippers,
smoking a fat cigar.
Yatta, yatta,
write the stinkin poem.
You want help sucker,
take this ball-peen hammer
and give yourself a shot
in the cranium.
Just write down some words,
your words
I ran out a long time ago
although I think
I still got something
about a pony and snow
and getting dark
but lemme check.

Oh, it's been used.

So just write.

RIDGES

Living between ridges
that string down
into the Virginias
and beyond.
Held all my life.
Enfolded even alone
in sleep's
other world.

Ridges the mother,
great snow-capped
mountains
the distant father.
This valley's
great good fortune
to be the heart
of nowhere.
Green innocence
and the sound
of rain on the roofs
of dreamers.

The other ridges
did not stop here
but one small mountain—Nittany
went no farther.
Arriving like a wave
that had no need
to reach the shore.

Staying to hold us
where we are.
Small paradise
(any paradise is small)
no way to say thank you
but to live
knowing you also chose
to stop here
recognizing home.

COLD SUN

(Arguing A Line of Poetry)

The sun
which she says
cannot be cold
touches her face
like an
old English ballad.

Leaves pressed
into books
will not
grow old.

The sun,
she says
cannot be cold.

There are
blind men
awash in the sea.
The salt
preserves
their souls.

The sun
she says
cannot be cold.

IF EVER

If ever you doubt
I am with you
close your eyes.

I will come to you
through the amber.

I will stay with you
poking holes
in the darkness.

For all of time
I will be your shadow,
forever touching
your shining face.

TURNIP

We slept
in the ground
long before you
knew us.

You fed us
to animals
so they could
survive the winter
before you
killed them.

From their
jagged history
The Chinese
learned
to talk
like a turnip.

When we
fall in love
there
is no romance
only the
great swelling
of flesh
the infusing
of flavor, smell,
purple bruise
of color,
big green leaves
not waving
but rising
like a flag
for the
dispossessed.

RAIN

The rain
luminescent
arriving with
little notice
from mist to tears
to waterfall.

No memory or
sense of duty
to those it never met.

But the windows
recognize the rain
weeping down their
glass squares.

Each drop lands
and finds its friends
which flow as one.
Then separately climb
back toward heaven.

As we must flow
and climb.

CHINA FLIGHT

So many times
the plane lifted
against the odds
after running almost forever
down the concrete
as though it could
get there that way.
Then slowly climbing
to inspect the heaven less skies
while the first needless directions
were given to the bored
from the bored
and the first
round of beverages
was carted down endless aisles
to the weary
by the weary.

Night coming.
Each of us left with
half a dream, bad water
and the feeling
we were going from
strange to strange.
Pu Dong the target
and the incomprehensible
country older than
consciousness,
older than beetles,
as old as pain.

We hung on
knowing less
each flight
about who
they could be.

Who we might
have been.

CLOTHES IN A CHEST OF DRAWERS

Dark inside
the drawers.
Secure.

Some clothes leave
from time to time
on the body
of a known entity
then return
perhaps tossed
into a basket
soap and water
warm spinning
until dry.

Each drawer
a small kingdom
one for his feet
one for when
he exercises
and so on.

Silence.
A lifetime
of certainty
except when
he opens a drawer
and you ride him
into the
unknown world.

NOVEMBER 10

Leaves fly
as they fall
fall as they fly.
Their story
and ours.

Walking
makes a sound.

Hills ache
with beauty.

And if you
take your life
in your hands
and hold it up
to the leaving light
it is made beautiful
so you can
take it
down again
and wear it.

CAN YOU GARGLE

Can you gargle
while you juggle?
Can you muddle
through the puddles?

Will the goon squad
spittoon squad
slobber slightly
if the moon nods?

Will the belch
of beering buffalos
cause static
in your tremolo?

If woulding could should
causes grief
can you face the world
not seek relief?

And then suppose
your bozo nose
snorts the hose
and bigly blows.

Can dormant doorknobs
dingly dong
without a doorbell
gone bong dong wrong?

Will warring weasels
driving diesels
steer toward helpless
gumming geezers?

So what was rightly wrought
dodging boom-bound buckshot
careening gleaners help a lot
crafty crows from Camelot.

ALL THAT JAZZ

This is the way
to come in the door.

The funk of those
who blew the music
into the black night,
not needing listeners.

Not needing anything
but what cleared
the neon
what stood up
as night gave way
to morning
like an execution
of broken dreams
blown through
a bari sax
into whatever
could hear it,

could simply
affirm its beauty.

B. BAXTER BEAR BOY

B. Baxter Bates Bruington bear
sometimes here and often there.
Sometimes bruin, sometimes hare
B. Baxter Bates Bruington bear.

B. Baxter you know the rest that fits here
puts his back to the clock, going back without fear.
What used to be then can now come quite near.
For B. Baxter Bates clap your paws and cheer.

B. Baxter whatever name you hold dear
paints in the studio, sits on his rear.
Furry B. Baxter, furry old bear
sits in the studio, hasn't a care.

Bruington bear's mind summons the past.
A life of just gadgets leaves him aghast.
No need for the virtually useless morass.
Happy our boy bear when locked in the past.

Baxter paints scenes from such secret places
where rabbits observe the starry paint spaces
and sometimes even an Amish oasis
inhabits the visions that B. Baxter chases.

and if you think "real" means hi-tech places
where money makes everyone put on false faces
then B. B. Bear can change your dim mind
a more-clever bear you will not often find.

FINALLY

For John Haag

Finally ready
for a teacher
the snow came
bringing what can
be learned from
white, gray,
silence and
the dark.

Deer moved
within that lesson
showing me
by their fragile lives
that beauty needs
no assurance.

Letting go.
Falling down
into snow.

A flake touching
my forehead
like a kiss
a baptism
or a
noiseless bell.

Then
a crow
at dawn
announcing
an old presence.

OLD TREES

The old trees
slowly cast
their shadows
across the field.

Tucking it in
for the evening.

The sleeping field
will not remember
what walks
through it
in darkness.

What walks
through
my sleep
cannot be
tucked in.

Empty trail
when I awaken.

SEVEN A.M. RAIN

Driving through
liquid glass
the first sun
hiding and asleep
I suddenly turn off
the obedient
windshield wipers
and become a bird
flying toward some
tree-top home
in love with
these small
splashes of life
just outside
my reach.

OCTOBER

Keep three things
October brings
we feel
but cannot know.

The transformed leaf.

The deeper breath
of lonely, joyful air.

The stars that hint
where smoke
from burning leaves
might go.

But find a fourth
and fifth and sixth
if one, two, three
must go.

The thinning light.

A pumpkin dance.

A snowflake falls
through shadow.

GOOD NEWS

If it is true
there will be
weddings
of squirrels
with birds.

Trees learning to fly

Art work
you needn't see
which could still
save your life.

Faces of
giant friendly flies
smiling
at the window.

Language from
the other side.

Seeds
you could plant
to grow yourself

no need
to fertilize
with ego

GRIEF

She arrives
a little while
after the death
and sits across
from me saying
I am the one
who must do this
the others have left
walking toward
the hills.

Her cloth bag
is emptied
on the carpet.
Light
inhales itself.
Darkness comes
without effort.

You must stay
with me.
You must learn
from me.

Your grief is
sunglasses
on a blind child.

Carry what you learn,
deep wound of
understanding,
farther than
the blue beyond.

Farther than
the yellow sun
can find its way.

THE SNOW

The snow
does not know
it is snow
until it
begins to melt.
Looks up,
learning from
the light.
Heat ignored.
Pock-marked by
the tracks of
rabbit and deer.
Becoming part
of things.

Gray remnants
of snow
on the edges
of the grass,
which also wants
its possibilities.

Perhaps it
would have
been better
to stay asleep
in the
book of snow.

(Within whose pages
lies my life.)

But the sun
Required I read
as frozen dreams
melt off the page.
Water attempting
wisdom.

MERWIN

He taught me more
than I could learn.
More than I had
a right to understand.

The silence of answers.

Tree branches
on a windy night
between the face
at the dark window
and distant lights.

The dark
he knew
crosses the light
again and again.

And Merwin
of course
was never there.
What was writing
came from
empty space.

No need for purpose.

Only the soundless
opening
of a door
to a place
I had never
imagined.

ON MY PROPERTY

As the mourning dove
walks the railing
its head nods
forward and backward
saying yes
to its own life.

Small pink tongue
of the squirrel
carefully draws
melted water
from the edge of
the onion snow.

No peasants
more perfect
than sparrows.
Sheer joy
of surviving.
The order established
with one's beak
rising together in
wing-blurred glory
into the blue sky
when they fight.

Fox gliding across
the hay field
like an exiled prince.
You don't need
to see me, it says,
I don't need
to see you.

On the wrist watch
of animals
the opossum
is the hour hand,
chipmunk
the second hand.

Starlings ugly
but when they
swarm the sky
in inexplicable flocks
moving in perfect unison
to an unknown
mind's command
their beauty appears
against the odds.

This property,
I pretend,
is mine.

I with names
for my
misunderstandings.

This, I say,
is a bird feeder.

THE DAY

The day
has begun
not knowing
its name.

In dark earth,
the garlic are
not sure
their family is
with them
but when
they are pulled
it is a reunion
and they age
together
with such joy,
braided
and touching.

Scent of
the linden tree
carried by
the wind
no concern
for beneficiaries.

Raccoon born masked
into the wrong life.

The house at night
whispers what
it has learned
to the closest house.

We are visitors.

Tiny space
among the
bounding stars.

BLUE TIDE TURNING

Living by
the ocean
too late to
be young.

First you went
to the ocean,
then the ocean
came to you.
The great blue
yawning as
it came.
Spitting pieces
of your plastic.

Lying on
its new bed
like an
uninvited lover.

I did not ask you
to come here
it says.
You did not
ask me
to join you.

Blue tide turns.

Nuns of
the deep
seek where
to go
when the sand
has exhausted
their leaping
toward the
same paradise
we had hoped for.

PHOTOSYNTHESIS

Leaves
alive with light.
Whose love
lets them
learn from light?
Leaning toward life.

Luminescent.

Green grows
into yellow
and back to green.

Translucent magic
by which
we are fed.

A glow lingers
long in the leaves
pushing the plant
to imagine
limas or
a little-leaf linden
and they then
imagine
their children
who do the same.

Lean toward the light.

BARN LIGHT

Purest white
finds the ground
against the astonishing
darkness.

The dark before
we intruded
thinking our
consciousness
the only one.

Barn light
cannot spread.
Beacon of loneliness.
Silence and
no one listening.
Stillness and
no one watching.

This is how
we fall asleep
final joy in which
the dark is spread-out
like a blanket
for the light
around our body
to finally rest.

FIREFLY

1.
Luminescent in the
darkening
hayfield theater.
Small pure light
saying here I am,
oh here.
Before I
see you clearly
you are gone.

Not fire,
not lightning
but a glow
from within.
May I glow
that way
extinguished
only to
flash again.

2.
But the empty moon
sails oblivious
as do we
reflecting light
we mistake
for our own
and the fireflies
stop for the night
to return
at the next dusk.

Here I am
oh here.

Firefly, firefly.
my kin
in my country.

DIAMOND WATER

When the heat,
at last,
cannot
recognize us
diamonds
become tiny
drops of water,
tears for what
we might
have become.

A WISH FOR YOU

One night
that seems
like every
other night
you can
somehow fly
and do so
far above
your home
and look down
seeing
your bit of existence
unwitting paradise
and having
flown
you return
to the ground
go back inside
and sleep
a kind of sleep
you never knew
existed.

At dawn
you awaken
in a nest.

SUMMER FRAGMENTS

Each blade of grass
spends its life
looking at others
thinking this is
the city
of my birth
but above it
the sky
calls and calls.

My deal
for the birds
is trade me
anything I have
in return for
your flight
but they just
fly away.

When you die
You go up
into the air
full of black particles
and you sing
in the deepest voice
you ever heard
becoming the voice
not the air.

Perhaps at our finest
we are like
the Brussels sprout
which waited
an eternity
to be understood.

Tough knot with
a big heart.

WHERE

Had the hours
no place for her?

Empty map
whose lines run
through my face.

Did the sky need
no more
small stars?

No tree
marked for her?

When she passed
did we fail?

Finally, it
came to ashes
and a bitter tongue.

The dead leave
no trace
and the living
are left with
terrible theatre
and a cup
of black water.

MERMAID

There is no need
for your promise.
You give me
stuffed peppers
and suggestions,
knowing me
more than I do.

There is no need
to say what
overtakes our lives
the pushing and pulling
in us
and when
I hear you
calling out in sleep
to what
wants your cells to
dance faster and faster,
I touch the many blankets
that cover you
and make the promise
made by old men
who have slowly
found out
the price
the light pays
to shine each day
and to keep holding
so long
so very long
against the dark.

DRIVING HOME IN THE DARK

The road seems
smaller now,
country road
with animals
who own everything
but this
asphalt strip,
watching not
understanding.

Small bit
of road noise
interrupting
the silent darkness
that can almost
rule
the light.

Rushing thoughts
in a machine
that will go
without purpose.

High beams
show only how little
I belong here.

From a slightly
open window.
spirits of the night
ask what I want.

Painted lines
try and save me.

Curves promise
a path to my bedroom
where I sleep alone
facing up

to who I am
as I both move
and stay
in place
while the night
grows darker
than I ever
thought it could.

WE ARE HELD

by our own
restless arms.
Sometimes
by others
or by the wildly
unimaginable
dark space
of the universe,
which, itself,
is held by
nothing.

Craving
connection
against our will.
The only way
on the only road.
Wrapping
into a circle
life that seemed
to be
a straight line.

Those who
would be free
sometimes
thrash at night
listening to the
whisper of trees
whose arms wrap
the starry sky.

Longing
to be held
by whatever
will hold them,
whatever realizes
this small here
is where
I reside.

VISITOR

Sun, sky and soil.

Blue skies
(smiling at me).

The contrails of jets,
graffiti of the sky,
quickly disappear.

No path.

Below,
cars like
schools of fish
rush toward
whatever is next
but then the lights
are switched on
in the infinite
and we begin to
float in it,
as a drunken poet
once floated
in a boat
whose direction
no longer mattered.

SUPPOSE

Suppose the dream
comes first
finding its own
amber way.

Suppose the things
you need to know
are tomatoes on
the snaking vine,
which must be
plucked in
such a way
the hand who
claims them
will never
be the same.

Suppose
the mouse
smugly
tells you
the plan
in which
you are
not included.

Suppose the
traffic noise
on the far interstate
becomes the
sound of death.

LONG TIME COMING

A dying king
tells the animals
he approves of them
as a final act
of dominion,
(as it says in
the black book).

Bacteria
along for the ride.

Flies in love
with their air.

Small moving things
crawling toward
their destiny.

What of them?

Any room left
 for what hides
in tall grass
or deep in the
nest of starlings?

Will we ever
learn to speak
as they do?

Waiting for the beauty
a long time coming.
Unrecognizable child
walking toward us
down the road,
the touched forehead
of the saved
never saved
by only ourselves.

MEMORY

There may have been
other ways
to get here
but this is how
the trail was lit.

This is how
the cards came out,
the queen of hearts
winking,
the king of spades
looking
straight ahead
with disdain.

This is how
the bread
was baked
but no one knows
how the yeast
did its work.

We rise,
sometimes
against our will,
like a seed
that finds out
who it is
after the
flower falls
and the fruit
emerges.

Each of us
covered with
the skin
of imperfection.
Small dance
that came

from somewhere
farther than
the next
interstate exit,
Moon of memory
raging against
the dark.
And finally
we see
just in time
what has
happened
and who
we are.

Geoffrey Godbey is a consultant, speaker, and Professor Emeritus in the Department of Recreation, Park and Tourism Management at Penn State University. The author of ten books and over 100 articles concerning leisure, work, time use, aging, recreation and parks, tourism, health and the future, he is the past President of the Academy of Leisure Sciences.

His career as a poet has included being published in *The Nation, The World and I, Malahat Review,* forty other literary magazines, and online in numerous outlets. He has published three chapbooks of poetry: *The Midget on a Bicycle* from Mansfield Press, *Finding Home* from Finishing Line Press and *Past That, Still There* from Finishing Line Press. He was a Festival Poet for the Central Pennsylvania Festival of the Arts and has given readings at many locations.

Previously a faculty member at the University of Waterloo in Ontario, Canada, Godbey has undertaken research for the American Association of Retired Persons, the US Forest Service, the National Recreation Foundation and the Robert Wood Johnson Foundation. He has been a consultant to the National Science Foundation, State Government of Sao Paulo, Brazil, US Department of the Interior, as well as many advertising agencies and public and private recreation, park and tourism organizations. Godbey has testified before committees of the United States Senate and the President's Commission on Americans Outdoors. A frequent public speaker to diverse groups, he has given invited presentations in twenty-four countries.

He also advised and was the spokesperson for Hampton Inn's Year of 1,000 Weekends campaign as well as serving on Hilton Hotel's Leisure Time Advocacy Board. From 2002-2004, Godbey helped develop the LifeTrail, a series of stretching and strengthening stations for older adults, for Playworld Systems, Inc. He was the Sir Yue-Kong Pao Visiting Professor at the Asia Pacific Center for the Study of Leisure, Zhejiang University, China for three years.

A book he co-authored with Dr. John Robinson entitled *Time for Life—The Surprising Ways Americans Use Their Time* was published by Penn State Press. Godbey completed a five city study of the relationships between use of leisure and health among older adults. Several of his books have been translated into Chinese, Korean, and Spanish.

Godbey has written for or been extensively quoted by a wide variety of academic journals and popular periodicals including *American Demographics, Prevention, Modern Maturity, Issues in Science and Technology, Public Opinion, American Journal of Preventive Medicine, Social Research, The Futurist, Journal of Leisure Research, Leisure Sciences, Annals of Tourism Research, Journal of Travel Research, Leisure Studies, The World and I, American Enterprise, Hospitality Research Journal, Parks and Recreation, World Tennis*, and many others.

Interviews and summaries of Godbey's writings have appeared in a number of mass media outlets including *US News and World Report, Newsweek, Time, Reader's Digest, The Economist, The Today Show, Good Morning America, CBS Morning Show, New York Times, Glamour, Psychology Today, Wall Street Journal, USA Today, Washington Post, Modern Maturity, the Chronicle of Higher Education, Cosmopolitan, Redbook, The Utne Reader, NBC Evening News with Tom Brokaw, CNN News, The ABC Evening News with Peter Jennings* and many others.

www.ingramcontent.com/pod-product-compliance
Lightning Source LLC
Chambersburg PA
CBHW020341170426
43200CB00006B/455